RUTH

Also by Olajumoke Adenowo

Non-Fiction

Child of Destiny

Covenant Forces

Life Spring (The Mother's Prayer Manual)

Designed for Marriage

Mysterious Seed

Appointment with Destiny

Fiction

Beyond My Dreams

RUTH

STRATEGIC WISDOM TO OVERCOME THE IMPOSSIBLE

(BOOK TWO)

KINGDOM DYNAMICS FOR THE MARKETPLACE

OLAJUMOKE ADENOWO

KINGDOM DYNAMICS FOR THE MARKETPLACE (BOOK TWO)

RUTH: Strategic Wisdom To Overcome The Impossible

ISBN 978-978-57390-2-2

Book Production, Design, & Printing:
Infospektra Publishing

Unless otherwise indicated, all scriptures are taken from the King James Version (KJV).

Contents

INTRODUCTION

This is the second book in a three-volume series on important Kingdom dynamics for the marketplace. The principles discovered and examined in these books are meant to be gleaned from the very unusual lives of Rahab, Ruth, and Tamar, three special women listed in the lineage of Jesus as recorded by Matthews in the Bible.

The first book in this series, *Rahab: Strategic Wisdom for Quantum Change,* was a study on Rahab and a detailed exploration of strategies she utilized which led eventually to her recognising the opportunity sent by God through the Israeli spies and grasping it intentionally. This ultimately caused her to make the leap from being accursed to becoming a part of the covenant laid out by God for Israel and, unbelievably, a matriarch in the ancestry and lineage of King David and our Lord Jesus. It is an astounding read and one which is sure to lift the veil over your eyes, cause you to align yourself strategically, and cause an evolution to begin in you. Do all you can to get it.

In this second volume, we would be looking into the life of Ruth and mining many strategies not covered in the first book. Having spent years actively involved in ministry and in the corporate world, I see these strategies playing out over and over again, and being of benefit even to those who are not professing Christians. Principles are principles after all and, like the law of gravity, work irrespective of one's belief system. In this series, therefore, we would be examining a few of these universally applicable principles. As we do, it is my hope that we would discover invaluable nuggets needed to propel us forward and upwards in our assignments, careers, and in the marketplace.

Ruth went from being a stranger in a foreign land to becoming part of God's chosen people, a woman of eternal honour, and one grafted into the lineage of Jesus like Rahab was.

Be inspired as you read!

And Ruth said, Intreat me not to leave thee, or to return from following after thee: for whither thou goest, I will go; and where thou lodgest, I will lodge: Thy People Shall Be My People, And Thy God My God.

Ruth 1:16

Chapter 1

OVERCOMING THE IMPOSSIBLE

An Ammonite or Moabite shall not enter into the congregation of the Lord; even to their tenth generation shall they not enter into the congregation of the Lord for ever: Because they met you not with bread and with water in the way, when ye came forth out of Egypt; and because they hired against thee Balaam the son of Beor of Pethor of Mesopotamia, to curse thee.
Deuteronomy 23:3-4

This book is about Kingdom principles which can be studied and applied in our individual assigned sectors. We will, therefore, focus to an extent on practical, everyday examples considering how robust our lives are, with special regard to individuals especially (majorly women) who may find it hard to compartmentalise one area of their lives in respect to others.

I am amazed at Ruth's tenacity and courage. She inspires me no end. The Moabites, of which she was a part of, had a curse from God hanging over their lives. God had placed a curse on the Ammonites and the Moabites and had clearly stated why:

> *... Because they met you not with bread and with water in the way, when ye came forth out of Egypt; and because they hired against thee Balaam the son of Beor of Pethor of Mesopotamia, to curse thee.*
> **Deuteronomy 23:4**

Some rabbis argue that the curse held only for male Moabites and not for the females. But in my book on David, *Appointment With Destiny: The Path to the Throne*, you will realise this issue was a huge one generations after and affected both sexes. Its existence was well acknowledged. Yet Ruth not only managed to overcome the curse but overturned it in an unbelievable manner.

If man curses you, you can run to God for refuge.

Sometimes when things are not going well for a business and one has done all one knows to do, one's mind begins to engage in spiritual forensics. *What could the matter be?* It is not odd to consider the existence of a curse against the business by acts of omission or commission. Usually, the individual would expect that the curse, if any, originates from a man. But in Ruth's case, she was under no such illusion. She knew the God of the Israelites had cursed her and her people.

It was not a curse she had incurred through any fault of hers, yet she had to suffer for the sins of her forefathers, which is the same way inequities, policies that lead to inequities, or a lack of policies that would make for an equitable playing field affect us as individuals (especially women) in the marketplace. There are also national issues not of our making which we suffer.

If man curses you, you can run to God for refuge. But if God curses you, to whom do you go for a solution? The curse against Ruth was national and personal. On a personal level, it directly impinged on her worship.

An Ammonite or Moabite shall not enter into the congregation of the Lord; even to their tenth generation shall they not enter into the congregation of the Lord for ever...
Deuteronomy 23:3

God made it clear Ruth could not worship in His temple. This in essence meant she was not welcome in His presence. It could be equal to hearing someone say "I don't want to see you!" or "Get out of my sight!" Rejection doesn't get any worse than that. Then when He now says, "Not only do I not want to see you, your descendants also should stay away from me till the tenth generation," I don't know about you, but from a modern standpoint that seems pretty harsh.

Yet Ruth, this young damsel, overcame these and was welcomed in. She also went on to become a grandmother to one from whom the One who cursed her would be born! If she could accomplish this, I really don't know what obstacle is impossible for us to overcome.

I am encouraged and inspired by her story and know that neither you nor I have such obstacles stacked against us today. For whatever obstacles we face, God's presence is accessible to us by the blood of the Lamb. What an awesome privilege we have by the sacrifice of Christ! There are no barriers we cannot overcome and scale through, irrespective of whether they are specific to our businesses or careers, or are communal curses like recessions, depressions, or famine.

... besides a desire to please God, ... there are principles that bring deliverance if engaged.

It is not recorded throughout the book of Ruth that she actively prayed at all times. Did you get that? Without constantly engaging in prayer, which some of us believe is the only key, Ruth prevailed. This simply tells us that besides a desire to please God, which she had, there are principles that bring deliverance if engaged. While miracles are divine interventions which are sovereign acts of God, principles are laid down tenets that, if applied, deliver predictable results.

We can apply certain principles and expect certain results. Prosperity or success in any field answers to principles. The Kingdom of God is based on principles. Principles can be learnt. It is my hope that as we stay receptive, we would learn important principles from this young woman who prevailed and had her story changed, despite having unimaginable odds stacked against her.

Chapter 2

IN SEARCH OF BREAD

Now it came to pass in the days when the judges ruled, that there was a famine in the land. And a certain man of Bethlehemjudah went to sojourn in the country of Moab, he, and his wife, and his two sons.
Ruth 1:1

I love the Word. As I study deeply stories and passages in the Bible, I am amazed to discover hidden truths not easily discernible from the surface. The story of Ruth is one example. Before we delve in let's have an overview of what transpired as written in scriptures.

Now it came to pass in the days when the judges ruled, that there was a famine in the land. And a certain man of Bethlehemjudah went to sojourn in the country of Moab, he, and his wife, and his two sons. And the name of the man was Elimelech, and the name of his wife Naomi, and the name of his two sons Mahlon and Chilion, Ephrathites of Bethlehemjudah. And they came into the country of Moab, and continued there. And Elimelech Naomi's husband died; and she was left, and her two sons. And they took them wives of the women of Moab; the name of the one was Orpah, and the name of the other Ruth: and they dwelled there about ten years.

And Mahlon and Chilion died also both of them; and the woman was left of her two sons and her husband. Then she arose with her daughters in law, that she might return from the country of Moab: for she had heard in the country of Moab how that the LORD had visited his people in giving them bread.
Ruth 1:1-6

... their cultures and instructions for daily living would come from Him.

When God brought the children of Israel out of the land of Egypt, he intended that they be distinct in their purpose and lifestyle. Unlike other nations of the earth, they would have no king: He would be their God: their cultures and instructions for daily living would come from Him. Israel was to be a true theocracy.

Moses acted as a guide to the people and, after he was gone, Joshua took over. When Joshua passed on, we see the Lord raising judges over the land of Israel to guide them in His way. Many times, when calamity befell the nation, it was a reflection of their turning away from precepts set by God.

In the verses above, we see there was a famine in the land, Bethlehemjudah, and the situation looked truly dire and desperate. Bethlehem means The House Of Bread, and Judah means Praise. In essence, the people were hungry in the house of bread, same as so many are today. We keep hearing of scarcity in nations and yet some are doing quite well. Is there really no bread? Or is access to bread not open to all?

It is in the midst of this that Elimelech, an indigene of Bethlehemjudah in Israel, chooses to leave the House Of Bread and God's people to go in search of bread. He chooses Moab, a land considered accursed by God, and there settles to build a life with his family.

THE ASSIGNED LOCATION

After some years in Moab, Elimelech dies along with his two sons, Mahlon and Chilion. Naomi the widow who has also lost her two sons chooses to return to Israel soon after.

> *Then she arose with her daughters in law, that she might return from the country of Moab: for she had heard in the country of Moab how that the LORD had visited his people in giving them bread.*
>
> **Ruth 1:6**

From the verses read earlier, we find the reason for Elimelech and his family leaving Israel was bread. Also, the reason for Naomi's return to Israel was also bread. This is a simple story but full of lessons. There are so many who have moved out of divinely ordained locations for no other reason than 'bread'.

I am not saying all forms of relocation are in error, but for Elimelech and his family it was a grievous choice. Not everyone moved away from Israel during the dearth, and we are not told that those left behind died as a result of the famine. So, ultimately, there was a way out for those who chose to stay in Israel.

Bread is important; let's not make light of it. Bread is the staff of life, and without it man would die. But Jesus said:

> *And Jesus answered him, saying, It is written, That man shall not live by bread alone, but by every word of God.*
>
> **Luke 4:4**

We are not meant to be motivated by 'bread' but by divine instruction.

And by this he meant, while bread is important, man's existence will not be based on physical forms of bread alone. There is another resource which can produce the bread you desire, and if you don't carry this resource with you wherever you are, it doesn't matter where you relocate to, true sustenance would still be elusive. What is this resource that births bread and other resources? The word of God. Man shall not live by bread alone but by every word *from the mouth of God.*

The answer to famine for Elimelech and his family was not necessarily in relocating to Moab but in hearing the *Rhema* (divine instruction from God). We are not meant to be motivated by 'bread' which can mean many things. It can be higher salaries, prestige, perks, statuses, more profit, a better relationship, a thriving location, a better paying job. Kingdom people don't take decisions based on 'bread'. We take decisions based on our God-given purpose. Kingdom people don't take on jobs, they take on assignments.

A job is not merely about a remuneration but about your transformation. Except by divine orchestration as evidenced in God sending Joseph, Daniel, Mordecai, and Esther to a strange land, of which they had no choice, our decision to leave a location must be by divine instruction, as seen in the case of Jacob. Although he was fleeing his brother's wrath, yet he met with God who endorsed his journey at Bethel. Isaac asked God in times of famine 'Should I move?' and God said 'No.' God then gave Isaac a business strategy, Irrigation, which helped in his overcoming the environmental challenges.

We should not move merely for economic exigencies. What beckons may look attractive but is it God? Are there relationships that you have lost because of 'bread'? How many times have you changed jobs because of 'bread' and failed to realize a job is not merely about what you can get but about being where God

A job is not merely about a remuneration but about your transformation.

desires you to be at the right time? As an employer of labour, I always say to my team "No matter how good the remuneration here is, the best value you derive from my firm, my company, my foundation is not the pay, but the person you become." If you give your best to serving another and thus learn in the process, even if the job is taken away, they cannot take away what you have learnt and the person you have become.

We are only meant to transition or relocate from one state to another because God says so. We go from one relationship to another, one job to another at His command, and not by external stimuli. We make choices, not for things that are transient and will fade, but for things which will bring us closer to our destiny.

Know where you are to be. Stay where you are sent. It is very dangerous to miss the location that God has assigned you to. I have learnt provision and location are linked. You cannot separate one from the other. If you want provision, make sure your location is right. It is possible to be praying for an answer in the wrong place when all the while the answer is waiting where you ought to be. *Are you where you are supposed to be?*

Kingdom people don't take on jobs, they take on assignments.

God told Abraham to go to Mount Moriah to sacrifice Isaac. It would be a three-day journey. It was inconvenient. It was tasking. It was a lengthy journey. The time span was long enough to make him rethink his actions and possibly choose not to obey God. Yet he kept going.

Can I not just stop at any mountain? Like Sinai? Is it not just a high ground God wants? Must it be Moriah? Am I sure I heard right? Do I really have to do this? Yet he kept going.

When he finally arrived at the mount after a long journey, weary in body and soul, he bound and prepared to slaughter Isaac, slaughter his laughter, slaughter his future generation, slaughter his legacy, kill his hope. But God said "Stop. I have provided a ram caught in a thicket by the horns."

Do you think the ram got there the minute Abraham wanted to slaughter Isaac? No. I believe God had provided the ram beforehand and sent it to a certain mountain called Moriah. When the ram was settled there, God told Abraham to go to Moriah.

Some of us would choose to go to London instead of Lagos and then complain we can't get a good job in the UK. Or, anytime a company downsizes you are the first to get laid off no matter how hard you work and how great your appraisal is. Have you ever asked if your location is right? I say this now to singles, you stay on the streets of Chelsea in New York believing God for a wife or husband and God says he or she is in Accra, Ghana.

Right there on the mount, Abraham discovered God as Jehovah Jireh which is interpreted to mean "In the mount of the Lord, the provision of the Lord shall be seen."

And Abraham called the name of that place Jehovahjireh: as it is said to this day, In the mount of the LORD it shall be seen.

Gen. 22:14

I have learnt provision and location are linked.

Favour and provision are tied to where you are meant to be. Business opportunities, a boss who is a great mentor, your dream job are all in the location God has prepared for you. You may simply need to relocate to where you are assigned.

THE POWER OF PRAISE

Isn't it amazing that the place departed from was named Bethlehemjudah? (The House of Bread and Praise!) This is the only place in the Bible where you find Bethlehem is used as one with Judah. They were in the land of bread where, if they praised God, the revelation that would lead to provision would have been released.

Even when business is bad and the job gets tough, there are several keys that deliver victory in the face of seeming, imminent defeat. Sacrificial giving is one, the power of rejoicing exuberantly and dancing before the Lord, worship and praise, prophetic proclamations from a bona fide prophet, engaging a fast for *greater clarity*, *accuracy* (Fasting doesn't change God. It changes **us**) is yet another. We need a whole book on these mysteries that deliver victory.

Is it possible for there to be famine in the house of bread? When it looks that way, your key is praise. Even when all the signs point to a famine, God still leaves us with a key – praise! When business is tough in the land of plenty, switch to worship. Whenever the prophecies spoken over your business seem not to be coming to pass, you don't relocate or run away. What you do is stay in the land of 'bread', and relentlessly face the 'famine' with praise.

Let the high praises of God be in their mouth, and a two-edged sword in their hand; To execute vengeance upon the heathen, and punishments upon the people; To bind their kings with chains, and their nobles with fetters of iron; To execute upon them the judgment written: this honour have all his saints. Praise ye the LORD.

Psa. 149:6-9

I pray for you that as you choose to actively engage God in praise where He has assigned you, you will see the victory He has commanded and you will be greatly comforted.

Chapter 3

REVIEWING FOUNDATIONS

And Elimelech Naomi's husband died; and she was left, and her two sons. And Mahlon and Chilion died also both of them; and the woman was left of her two sons and her husband.
Ruth 1:3, 5

The story of Elimelech and his family is a sad one. If we are to make quick judgements, we could say the losses experienced were a direct result of stepping out of the place assigned to the people of God. If we go deeper, however, we discover some odd circumstances.

Long before they made the move to Moab, Elimelech (meaning The King) and Naomi (Sweetness) had two sons. They were named Mahlon and Chilion. Mahlon means Invalid. Chilion means Sick. This might have been the result of their being weak and fragile when they were born. How powerful our confessions are. If only one parent had been astute enough as Jacob had been.

Then they journeyed from Bethel. When they were still some distance from Ephrath, Rachel went into labor, and she had hard labor. And when her labor was at its hardest, the midwife said to her, "Do not fear, for you have another son." And as her soul was departing (for she was dying), she called his name Ben-oni; but his father called him Benjamin.
Genesis 35:16-18

Racheal, after a very difficult birth in which she felt life ebbing from her, looked at the baby who seemed to be the immediate cause of her pain, sorrow, and subsequent death and named him Ben-oni (Son of My Sorrow). Her husband, Jacob, was in deep mourning and deep distress, and like Rachael, he had a reason to speak words which reflected his pain. But in spite of the fact that this son seemed to have cut short the life of the one he loved, he chose to do something different. He overturned the dire prophecy in the name given and renamed his son Benjamin, (Son of My Right Hand), prophesying a destiny that defied present circumstances.

How powerful our confessions are.

Rahab's parents also named their daughter after a great envisioned destiny - Enlargement. She went ahead to fulfil this prophecy despite seemingly insurmountable odds and was grafted into God's covenant people and, ultimately, the lineage of Christ.

Naomi and Elimelech, however, named their sons after their perceived circumstances – Invalid and Sickly. Every instance when the boys were summoned or mentioned, sickness and weakness were also being invoked upon them. "Sickness, Weakness, come and dine," Naomi would say. "Sickly and Weak come to the farm with me," Elimelech would call. This went on and on until the names the boys were called grew mightily and prevailed. What a tragedy.

So mightily grew the word of God and prevailed.
Acts 19:20

Words, good or evil, grow and prevail. Unfortunately, I believe they became what they were called. After a while, Mahlon and Chilion died as young men, within ten years of moving to Moab. Despite the advantages of the covenant, they died prematurely and without a legacy.

And Elimelech Naomi's husband died; and she was left, and her two sons. And they took them wives of the women of Moab; the name of the one was Orpah, and the name of the other Ruth: and they dwelled there about ten years. And Mahlon and Chilion died also both of them; and the woman was left of her two sons and her husband.
Ruth 1:3-5

THE POWER OF WORDS

Death and life are in the power of the tongue:
and they that love it shall eat the fruit thereof.
Proverbs 18:21

As we study Naomi, the mother of these boys, we see a pattern begin to emerge. Naomi understood the power of words perfectly. The few times she spoke passionately in scriptures her words were deliberately chosen and reflected what she felt. She didn't seem to have learnt from what had befallen Mahlon and Chilion, or she just didn't make a connection between the boys' names and their fate. Or, perhaps like some of us, she just believed in "…saying it the way I see it."

Example 1: When she returned to Israel and was called Naomi (Sweetness), she rejected it and asked to be called Mara, (Bitterness), reflecting the intense bitterness of her heart.

Words, good or evil, grow and prevail.

So they two went until they came to Bethlehem. And it came to pass, when they were come to Bethlehem, that all the city was moved about them, and they said, Is this Naomi? And she said unto them, Call me not Naomi, call me Mara: for the Almighty hath dealt very bitterly with me.
Ruth 1:19-20

This was a clear indication that she knew the meaning and importance of the names of individuals as evidenced in her calling herself Mara (Bitter) instead of Naomi (Sweetness). Perhaps she had no choice in the issue of what her sons were christened? Perhaps Elimelech didn't have the understanding she had and his will prevailed? Could she not have called her boys pet names that counteracted the evil invocations?

Many mothers have their own private names for their children. If we wait on God for a way out, isn't it possible that there is wisdom provided for different issues? For women in patriarchal societies where they have little to no choices, for businesses where the accountants and internal auditors insist on dire prognoses?

God is faithful and can be counted on. He always provides help in times of need.

Example 2: When Naomi spoke to her daughters-in-law as she prepared to return home, she spoke hard words.

And Naomi said unto her two daughters in law, Go, return each to her mother's house: the LORD deal kindly with you, as ye have dealt with the dead, and with me.
Ruth 1:8

God is faithful and can be counted on. He always provides help in times of need.

This is odd at first glance. Nowhere in the Bible or in most cultures around the world do you tell anyone "Go to your mother's house". The norm, even in Israel, was to mention the "father's house". The father was considered head, owner, and the primary representation of the family. Yet when Naomi told them to return to their mothers' houses, she meant two things:

- **"I am not your mother."**
  In other words, "Your mothers will be expecting and would be glad to see you both. Go to her bosom and find rest in her. Go find your mothers." Beyond telling them to return home, she was rejecting them and the relationship they insisted on having with her.

- **"I am not your mother."**
  In other words, "My motherhood is in vain. I was a mother but I have come away empty. I thought I was a mother. Where are my children? What do I have to show for motherhood? Go. I am not a mother. I am not your mother. I have anything to offer you."

When Naomi spoke these words she didn't realise she spoke hastily and would be entering into a different season where she would become a mother, not just to Ruth but to Obed and his siblings, her grandchildren. Unfortunately, she didn't trust or know God enough to believe a new beginning could occur. But despite Naomi's confession, Ruth's faith and tenacity prevailed and won a victory not only for herself but also for Naomi.

This is so encouraging. I rejoice, as you should, at the mercy of God. Keep your confessions of faith. Keep to it! Not only will you rejoice when your victory comes, but others who have lost hope will have cause to rejoice in your testimony.

Let us hold fast the profession of our faith without wavering; (for he is faithful that promised.
Hebrews 10:23

THE SEASON OF CONTRADICTION

The Chinese bamboo tree grows to a height of 17 feet. That's what you are told when you purchase it. You envision a mighty bamboo tree and build a gazebo that the huge tree will overshadow.

In the first year, you water and care for it, and it grows one inch.

In the second year, you water and care for it, and it grows one more inch.

In the third year, you water and care for it some more hoping to have different results, but it grows one more inch.

People are wondering what you are spending so much time working on. They can't see anything which justifies the time and effort invested. You are also beginning to doubt considering its been years now and this tree has only grown three inches.

You are becoming the laughing stock of the neighbourhood; the maize farmers have had corn stalks taller than your crops now for three consecutive years and you are still stuck with your itsy-bitsy tree. All you have to go on are the words you have been told. Mere words, just a promise, and the assurance that this is the way of this species of bamboo. The experiences of others who have walked on this same path also guide you.

Does this sound familiar? Can you see a parallel with your trials?

In the fourth year, you water and care for it, and it grows one more inch.

In the fifth year, you water and care for it, and it grows one more inch.

In the sixth year, you water it as you have always done. No special care or extra fertilisers. No extra words or confessions, nothing else. Just the same faithful care you always gave year in year out, even as weeds grew rapidly over it. Yet, in the sixth year, it grows seventeen feet at once! It grows higher than the corn growing and dying annually. It grows as tall as the palms rewarding their farmers with annual growth spurts. It grows higher than almost every other plant. All in one year!

Did it grow seventeen feet in ONE year? Or was it growing all along when it was not apparent to the eye? Were all the processes that created seventeen feet in one single year loading over a six-year period? Obviously! They were silently at work. If care had stopped at any time in previous years for the "unrewarding tree" it wouldn't have rewarded you with all the growth seen in the 6th year. This is the fight of faith!

We must learn to separate facts from truth. Facts are what is happening and what your eyes see. Truth is who God is and what He has said, His Word and His promises.

> *While we look not at the things which are seen, but at the things which are not seen: for the things which are seen are temporal; but the things which are not seen are eternal.*
> **2 Corinthians 4:18**

Truth is not what you see with your eyes, what you think or feel. Truth is the word of God (the unseen), is eternal, and dominates the seen realm. Facts are temporal or changeable and subject to the Truth. This is the good news and one we should never forget.

It's especially true in business, especially for professionals. For years, you seem to be building a reputation, building a name. Hardly anyone seems to notice. Sometimes all you have to go on is "The Lord revealed to me...." You teach on prosperity and people are thinking to themselves as they look at you, "Physician heal thyself." You're obeying and doing all you should yet it looks like you have accomplished nothing.

Facts are what is happening and what your eyes see. Truth is who God is and what He has said.

All of a sudden (or so it seems to the observer) there is an explosion and your name is on everyone's lips. People begin to take notice of you and want to be a part of your life. Those who have rejected you begin to see you as important. Like the bamboo tree, your time of manifestation has come. That's God in action.

If, however, you had stopped delivering world-class standards even in the days of being little, then the days of recognition would never have come. If those tough years of silent preparation had not been invested, the promotion would have led to humiliation. You would be handed jobs, assignments, contracts, problems you weren't prepared to handle, and all eyes would be on you. Unlike the days you were hidden, if you fail now it's no longer in private. Now, you have a huge audience.

Prepare now while you are waiting, for when preparation does not precede promotion, promotion leads to humiliation.

Listen, O isles, unto me; and hearken, ye people, from afar; The Lord hath called me from the womb; from the bowels of my mother hath he made mention of my name. And he hath made my mouth like a sharp sword; in the shadow of his hand hath he hid me, and made me a polished shaft; in his quiver hath he hid me…

Isaiah 40:1-3

Often, we pray against and accuse the enemy of what he has no part in. He isn't as powerful as we make him out to be. God takes responsibility for hiding His servants. In this excerpt from Isaiah above, we see the servant was prepared. Yet the Lord hid him (her). God is the One who is behind His own servant not 'blowing up!' Can you comprehend that? In this age of social media? Why would God do this? Surely He should know that blowing up is everything!

Stay prepared. Even though you think you are more than ready for recognition, keep doing your best consistently. Recognition is loading…

WATCH YOUR WORDS

Even though God was birthing something new, Naomi wasn't perceptive to the changes taking place. She spoke many words when leaving her daughters-in-law and to everyone who welcomed her when she returned to Israel.

In seasons of contradictions, success is only guaranteed if an important principle is followed: You watch your words. Watch your words, especially when you go through seasons you do not fully understand. Your actions or reactions are not about how you *feel.* Those periods are times to exercise your faith muscles and speak the Word in faith.

Like Naomi, there are some who are constantly critical when faced with the unexpected or undesired. They label their children Dullards in response to dismal academic or received reports. Others do the same with their businesses. I am not saying watching your words is easy. I am saying it is **necessary.**

We must do all we can to hold on to our profession of faith. Weeping may endure for a night but joy comes in the morning!

Who being the brightness of his glory, and the express image of his person, and upholding all things by the word of his power…
Hebrews 1:3

The verse above tells us God upholds all things by the *word* of His power. Not by the *power* of His words. This simply means all things are upheld by a word which contains the power needed to do the work. The word has to go *first*; it is the technology that communicates His power. You are created in the image of God.

And God said, Let us make man in our image, after our likeness: and let them have dominion over the fish of the sea, and over the fowl of the air, and over the cattle, and over all the earth, and over every creeping thing that creepeth upon the earth. So God created man in his own image, in the image of God created he him; male and female created he them.
Genesis 1:26–27

Watch your words, especially when you go through seasons you do not fully understand.

Furthermore, God gave mankind the ability to function in aspects of His divine nature.

And the LORD God formed man of the dust of the ground, and breathed into his nostrils the breath of life; and man became a living soul.
Gen. 2:7

When God breathed into man at creation, man became a living breathing spirit. Some translations render this verse -

"...and man became a ***speaking*** *spirit."*

The same ability you possess to criticise and tear down is the same ability you possess to build up and make whole.

The only organism that speaks apart from God is man. So, when you speak, child of God, let that speech count. It is a divine gift and a creative force. It can ruin your business. It can make your business. The same ability you possess to criticise and tear down is the same ability you possess to build up and make whole. It may be tough to do this when you don't see anything. But, as with the Chinese bamboo tree, even when you see *nothing*, just keep saying what God has said.

Maybe you feel like Naomi did and think you can't go on. "I've tried and tried. You're asking me to try again? What of all the years I have been trying? I am shutting down the business." This may just be the season of contradiction. We must keep *hope* (our trust in the nature and ways of God) alive, and also keep *acting* positively by keeping *faith* alive as we stay professing what God has said, and acting in accordance with our faith.

Let's not say what we see. Let's say what we *desire to* see. It is a season, and as is the nature of all seasons no matter how long, it will pass. Change is coming!

Chapter 4

COMFORT ZONES

And Ruth said, Intreat me not to leave thee, or to return from following after thee: for whither thou goest, I will go; and where thou lodgest, I will lodge: thy people shall be my people, and thy God my God.
Ruth 1:16

The lines above were spoken by Ruth at the intersection of an important season in her life. Like Rahab before her, she was faced with two choices and needed to make a decision about her future immediately. This was a weighty decision and not to be taken lightly. Should she return home to the life she grew up with, what was familiar, and the culture and customs she was accustomed to? Or should she follow Naomi, leave her world and gods behind, journey with her into a new world and into the unknown?

As business people, we are often called by God to leave our comfort zones. We are always presented with the choice to stay with the familiar, knowing full well all it offers has been explored, or venture outward into the unknown at God's behest believing that greater good awaits.

If you can't venture beyond the familiar, forget about doing anything great.

The only constant in the 'marketplace' is change. If you can't venture beyond the familiar, forget about doing anything great. If you can't embrace new ideas, new technologies, new strategies, forget about being an entrepreneur and succeeding in the marketplace. Alexander the Great said "Fortune favours the bold".

One distinguishing trait most business persons share is an appetite for risk. IF you are risk-averse, forget about being an entrepreneur. Please note that risk taking is different from recklessness. And while it is possible to mitigate risk to an extent, at the end of the day, you must still take the leap of faith. There are some afraid to take the first step because they want all the lights to be first green. Be very sure, as is often discovered when we step out into new ventures, everything does not always go as planned. Some of our plans fail. But they will be replaced with better plans! That's God's promise.

And we know that all things work together for good to them that love God, to them who are the called according to his purpose.
Rom. 8:28

God always has a better plan than we can imagine. You get to the shop you planned to lease and the landlord says it's no longer available. Wonderful. God has a better location! The bank promises you a loan. Then it suddenly asks for impossible conditions days to when you need the money. Trust me when I say this, God has a better plan.

Some of our plans fail. But they will be replaced with better plans! That's God's promise.

A Song of degrees. I will lift up mine eyes unto the hills, from whence cometh my help. My help cometh from the LORD, which made heaven and earth.
Psa. 121:1-2

Every time a door shuts, it's because He has a better door He has prepared. How far can we really see? How far can we really project the markets and the business climate? Let's trust God. He sees all. He knows what may look good now but will end in a loss. He always has a better plan.

Chapter 5

RELATIONSHIPS AND CHANGING SEASONS

And Ruth said, Intreat me not to leave thee, or to return from following after thee: for whither thou goest, I will go; and where thou lodgest, I will lodge: thy people shall be my people, and thy God my God.
Ruth 1:6

Ruth's decision wasn't helped by Naomi's reluctance to have her follow her. How do you follow someone who doesn't really want you to be with her? Someone who doesn't seem to see any value in you enough to want you around? Was she a burden which Naomi felt could weigh her down? If Naomi felt this way, would the land she was returning to be welcoming? If not, who would she turn to?

It recently struck me how young Ruth was at this time. She was referred to as a damsel by Boaz. The word Damsel expires at adolescence in the context of that society. She must have married in her teens as was common in those times and was still young as Orpah also must have been. This probably also informs why Naomi suggested they both still needed their mothers' care.

Naomi was too blinded by her grief and so embittered that she couldn't have received what God wanted at that moment. The one to wipe her tears away, give her a new lease of life, and restore her honour was the very person she was putting away. How did Ruth have such strength of conviction to insist on following a bitter older woman back to an unknown country where she (Ruth) had no support system? This young Moabite damsel said with such conviction:

Relationships are tools of intervention to change a trajectory. If God wants to bless and promote you, He will bring someone new into your life.

Intreat me not to leave thee, or to
return from following after thee:
for whither thou goest, I will go;
and where thou lodgest, I will lodge: thy people shall
be my people, and thy God my God.
Ruth 1:16

What a word! This was from the spirit, and like Jesus said to Peter, "Flesh and blood has not revealed this to thee." (Matt

16:17) If God had not intervened and made Ruth forcefully stake her claim to God's purpose, even though she didn't fully understand it, they both would have lost the opportunity to change the course of history. Her decision to go with Naomi affected her life, Naomi's, Israel's, and the history of Jesus.

Relationships are tools of intervention to change a trajectory. If God wants to bless and promote you, He will bring someone new into your life. Even as bleak as the outlook might seem, I am convinced that God is preparing a relationship for you to change the course of your trajectory. But we must be sensitive, watch our words, and not let our emotions stop God's purpose.

DISCERNING BRIDGES TO DESTINY

Every human being is made or unmade by relationships. I don't know when last God came down to help anyone in physical form. Everything He does, He does through human beings. And we all must relate to human beings.

Every human being is made or unmade by relationships.

The name Ruth means Female Friend. Isn't it amazing? The signs had always been there all along. Naomi's story would be changed, not by her Elimelech, or her two sons, but by Ruth, a female friend, who would bring out in Naomi the power of a kingmaker which she didn't know existed in her. A female friend would be Naomi's entrance to and reference in history, the reason her name would be recorded in the Bible.

As a female, you may have had terrible encounters with other women. Yet, it may still be a woman - who may not look or sound like it - who would be a blessing to you and bring that opportunity you have been dreaming of.

Naomi was meant to be a kingmaker. It is extremely important to note that kingmakers are not kings themselves and may never be kings, so they may not look like they possess what it takes to make you king or queen. But don't be deceived, their calling is simply to enthrone. They don't have to look or smell like it.

It is extremely important to note that kingmakers are not kings themselves and may never be kings, so they may not look like they possess what it takes to make you king or queen.

Ruth was more beautiful, more agile, more vibrant, and her future looked better than Naomi's somewhat. Yet she chose to bow and submit to this seemingly wretched woman. She served Naomi faithfully and humbly despite the shortcomings Naomi might have had. There is a posture needed to receive grace from a kingmaker. Ruth assumed that posture.

Let's examine the nuances of relationships in deeper detail, as they exist on so many different levels.

There are relationships with those who are high up and needed to assist you. Their positions would be revealed outwardly or by the help of the Spirit. Naomi occupied such a position. She would be the key to lifting Ruth up.

Some relationships are generational, transcending from father to son, mother to daughter. The king of Tyre, Hiram, had a relationship with David. He was the first to recognise and endorse him as a king. This is similar to the president of a nation being recognised as the de facto president by presidents of the United States of America, EU countries, etc, after a controversial election result.

David would have remained a local hero if Hiram had not sent ambassadors to him. At that time, Israel was no more than a tribe in the hills somewhere that the world didn't really find relevant, while Tyre was a super-power, especially in trade and commerce. Yet, Hiram recognised and endorsed David, and other kings had no choice but to follow suit. He even built David a palace! What is a king worth without a befitting palace?

And Hiram king of Tyre sent messengers to David, and cedar trees, and carpenters, and masons: and they built David an house.

2 Samuel 5:11

This relationship became generational after Solomon, David's son, was blessed by it after the death of David.

And Hiram king of Tyre sent his servants unto Solomon; for he had heard that they had anointed him king in the room of his father: for Hiram was ever a lover of David.
1 Kings 5:11

Hardly ever is this possible. This was completely divine. May God send us our Hiram in due season!

We all need endorsers. No matter how much you tout the fact that you are, you are not until an endorser who has the platform says you are. In every industry, there are kingmakers and gatekeepers. Endorsers must place their stamp of approval on you. Restaurant critics must write good reviews of your restaurant.

No matter how much you tout the fact that you are, you are not until an endorser who has the platform says you are.

Sometimes, the endorser is not just one important person but an agglomeration of unknowns. A queue forms outside a food stall in Manhattan despite the next stall selling the same product. Soon, others join the line because they see a queue. They imagine people can't be queuing for no reason!

In the movie industry, critics must rave about your movie. The right producer must handle your music, the right radio stations must play your single or no one hears it, a not-so-known but connected maven must refer people to your video on YouTube. The right journals must publish your work as an academic, and so on. I am sure you get my point.

Like Hiram, there are people God would send to endorse you. All they have to do is mention who you are and confirm what you can do to the right people, and soon everyone would be calling. They have a position and can approve of you and offer you their platform.

Hiram was a king, so it's not difficult to see him as a helper sent by God. But there are seemingly lowly bridges to destiny that people often overlook. These don't look like much and seem to have nothing to offer. Like Naomi may have looked to Ruth.

Naaman's maid who was a slave captured in battle is also a good example. I believe because she was treated well by her owners, she had the mental and emotional latitude to reveal there was a prophet in Israel who could provide the help they needed. If her stomach wasn't full, if she wasn't relatively content in her lot, if her own basic needs weren't met, and if she wasn't engaged in conversation regularly with her mistress, how would a captive slave girl suddenly blurt out that there was a prophet who could help her mistress' husband? Naaman and his family experienced prosperity in an unimaginable manner because they treated not just an employee, but a slave well.

How do you treat your employees? I know people who don't pay their employees what they are owed but fund their lifestyles and those of their mistresses directly from their businesses, with their accountants observing. The accountant superintends payments of the mistress' first-class tickets to the tune of thousands of dollars, and yet he has not been paid a fraction of the fare which he has earned through hard work and diligence.

Many people are in the quandary they are today because they have refused to honour the lowly. Some *seemingly* lowly people are **Gatekeepers.** They hold the keys to the doors you need to pass through. Some are sentries, gatemen, secretaries, personal assistants to CEOs you desperately want to connect with. These are people closest to the boss who you don't bother to acknowledge as you float into the boss' office.

Honour all men. The title someone holds may not accurately depict the power they wield.

NAVIGATING RELATIONSHIPS

I am sure everyone wants a mentor who is warm and nice. I don't think Naomi could be described as such all the time. A mentor's role in your life is dual: to teach you what you ought to learn, and to reveal how not to do things.

To tap into the blessings present in someone's life, you must honour the person and the anointing on them. Saul, either David knew it or not, was important to David's progress. David learnt first-hand what he should and shouldn't do as a king. He saw how Saul treated him with rabid envy and he didn't make that mistake when he became king. As he ruled, he empowered and celebrated his mighty men instead of feeling threatened.

How do you understand and handle appropriately each relationship that comes your way? Here are a few tips to help guide you.

Define Each Relationship Clearly

Don't play with or near a fire. You may fall in or be burned.

The married man who drops you off at home from the office every evening, what is his relationship with you? Is he just your back-to-home-from-work driver? If that's what both of you really believe, perhaps you may be safe. However, two adults in constant *proximity* over long periods cannot maintain a neutral relationship after a while. This is usually impossible. As a female, why not find a female to drop you off instead?

Honour all men (and women). The title someone holds may not accurately depict the power they wield.

As the Bible says, can you have fire in your bosom and not be burned? (Prov. 6:27) It is not possible. This is where many single ladies have been hurt. You are close to a gentleman. He defines you as a friend. You define him as a future husband. You both are obviously not on the same page. As a female, don't rush ahead of the man in developing a relationship or be quick to define it as something it is not. Protect your heart.

Have you read my work of fiction *Beyond My Dreams*? You should read it. In all modesty, there are timeless principles and lots of pointers in that book on the dynamics of male-female relationships.

Identify Coaches

Everyone needs someone in their corner who says "Sister, you can do it." Someone quick to commend and applaud you, and let you know when you have made mistakes. Have you ever seen a star athlete without a coach? We all need coaches. They may also be termed Mentors.

A mentor's role in your life is dual: to teach you what you ought to learn, and to reveal how not to do things.

Find someone who believes in you and has achieved something you admire or hope to accomplish. You need someone who can affirm you. Someone whose shoulders you can cry on, and who can still cheer you on as you shine.

Identify Collaborators

Collaborators are those willing to work with you to help build a purpose and achieve a common goal. These are people you build your core team around. Celebrate them, invest in them, and compensate them.

Also, avoid liaisons where you are neither ministering nor being ministered to. You must understand this. If this isn't the case, and growth isn't happening, you can have a cordial and more *distant* relationship. One in which you don't need to invest as much time and effort.

Identify Confronters

Many of us don't like confronters, but they are necessary to our growth. They identify your weaknesses and have the courage to face-off with you to make you confront areas in which you may be lacking. While we may prefer friendly confronters, those who seem very unfriendly or outright enemies have something to teach us by the hateful way they spew truth at us. I pray we have the maturity to extract truth from the vitriol.

… avoid liaisons where you are neither ministering nor being ministered to.

As you become more and more successful you are faced with fewer confronters. Everyone wants to be in your good books. No one wants to lose their relationship with you. Leaders are often surrounded by sycophants for this reason. Insecure leaders can't handle confronters. Anyone who tells them what makes them feel uncomfortable is labelled a hater. Unfortunately, they invariably fail because of this.

You need confronters on your team. Don't cut off those who disagree with you or tell you uncomfortable truths. Keep them around, cultivate them. Encourage them to stay truthful by not firing or punishing them overtly or covertly when they do.

Build up your team enough to confidently disagree with you. Don't be comfortable with being surrounded by a bunch of 'yes men'.

If you are a confronter, do so in love. Let your affirmation exceed your condemnation. Human beings remember criticism four times as much as they remember praise. Therefore, affirm a lot more than you criticise.

Identify Competitors

I know someone whose husband said, "If I see you are getting richer than me I will sabotage you. It's alright for you to prosper. Just don't prosper as much as I do." This is scary but a reality for some in marriage. They don't have spouses who are really on their teams to help them fulfil their potential.

Don't cut off those who disagree with you or tell you uncomfortable truths.

To be able to lead, get involved in and inspire the best performance from all in your team, and deliver on specific goals is a key asset. Unfortunately, there are some who live like everyone is a competitor.

You need allies. The ability to be able to collaborate is key. You will need people who are with you in non-competitive relationships, people you can work with on projects who possess competencies you may lack or your core team may not have.

Identify Seasons

Most relationships we find ourselves in last for a season. A few, however, span a lifetime. Some relationships are transactional or set up for specific projects, some become long-term associates or are employees just passing through, irrespective of how much you invest in them or how much like Jesus you are. Remember Judas who was Jesus' employee? They move on because their goals are not aligned with yours.

I know some who are hurt, resentful, or refuse to let go when a relationship has outlived its purpose. Some, women especially, who are new in business take these separations and sometimes outright betrayals really hard at first. But we have to learn not to internalise other people's decisions. It is usually not personal. You met these individuals because of a purpose. Perhaps the purpose is over. Don't be upset when that season ends. Learn which relationships to hold on to or which to let go of.

Also, don't keep anyone around for sentimental reasons either when you know you should let them go. This is detrimental to them and to the business. Let God guide you always.

Chapter 6

BECOMING SELF-SUFFICIENT

And Naomi had a kinsman of her husband's, a mighty man of wealth, of the family of Elimelech; and his name was Boaz.
Ruth 2:1

The second chapter of Ruth opens with an introduction to Boaz. He is a relative to Naomi and very wealthy. This is where one would expect the story would take a different turn.

Naomi would not be alone and without help when she returned to Israel. Her problems were automatically over and her needs automatically met. Why? She had a relative who was very very wealthy. Isn't God good? All the women had to do was stretch out their hands and Boaz would help.

I have seen this sense of entitlement at play, especially in some social settings in Africa where people feel a rich relative 'owes' them. Frankly, it's disgusting. His wealth is his, her wealth is hers, and they are each at liberty to dispose of what they have as they will.

Naomi and Ruth were not entitled, kinsmen beggars. They chose to fend for themselves. Despite being at the very bottom of society, a widow and a damsel with no male relative to help, we find them choosing to tow a different path. I find it hard to describe in modern terms how bereft of support they were. In ancient Israel they were destitutes. But Ruth took it upon herself to step out and source for provision.

LEARN THE CULTURE

Ruth's choices were limited. Of course, she could have turned to the oldest profession in the world – prostitution – or become a beggar. She chose neither but chose to glean instead. Gleaning was, at the time, a welfare package. It was later made into law by God where the wealthy (including the stingy) were forced to do a bit in providing for the poor. Based on what it entailed, the poor could legitimately go into the fields of the rich during harvest to pick up whatever the reapers left behind.

I have seen this sense of entitlement at play especially in some social settings in Africa where people feel a rich relative 'owes' them.

When thou gatherest the grapes of thy vineyard, thou shalt not glean

it afterward: it shall be for the stranger, for the fatherless, and for the widow.
Deut. 24:21

I find it interesting and instructive that Ruth, despite being new to Bethlehem, had studied the mores and ethics of this new and foreign culture and knew what to do to care for herself and her mother-in-law so they wouldn't go hungry or die. It showed she must have been amiable, receptive, adaptable, and cultivated new relationships through which she sourced information. These are traits every business owner needs in a new environment or industry.

A SENSE OF ENTITLEMENT

There are no unimportant details in the Bible. Why did the Bible mention Boaz as being of great wealth? Here's one reason I believe. It is a message for those who seem to have a sense of entitlement. "I have a wealthy brother who has done nothing for me." "I have a rich aunt who hasn't helped me out like I expect her to." "I asked for help. After all my father did for her, how could she turn me down?" "My friend has more than enough to go around. Why can't she spare some for me?"

There are people who go around keeping tabs on who they think they can get a favour from. Many drop subtle hints to get what they want. Some enter into relationships not because they value the individual but because of what they hope to gain. You don't love the other party and know you have no intention of ever being fully committed to them, yet you give out favours because of what you hope to get. It's defined in the dictionary as prostitution.

We need to take responsibility for our own future. We are not to expect reward where we have contributed no value for which a demand has been made and upon which the beneficiary has agreed a set remuneration.

We need to take responsibility for our own future. We are not to expect reward where we have contributed no value for which a demand has been made and upon which the beneficiary has agreed on a set remuneration. Merely showing up at work from 8am to 5pm does not entitle you to a pay. You should do all you can to deliver value. If the organisation does not set goals for you, study the objectives of the organisation and set goals for yourself based on those objectives. Act like this is your own business and your own cost centre, making sure it's efficient and the value you give the firm is more than you extract from it.

In society, the rich treat people with respect when they know you are not fixated on their wealth. You bring something of value to the table and are not ashamed of what you have or earn. This earns you a lot of respect and that was Ruth's ethos.

Some actually have a sense of entitlement towards even God! They spend time praying, scheming, and plotting on a particular path without seeking God's direction. They later expect God to fall in line with their plans. Was it God's will for you? Has He led you in that direction? Or are you simply fixated on a person, place, or purpose He hasn't sent you to?

> *Therefore speak unto them, and say unto them, Thus saith the Lord GOD; Every man of the house of Israel that setteth up his idols in his heart, and putteth the stumblingblock of his iniquity before his face, and cometh to the prophet; I the LORD will answer him that cometh according to the multitude of his idols…*
> **Eze. 14:4**

When you fixate your heart on a person, place, process, or path and then later come to God asking for His help, there is very little He can do. You will be unable to hear Him above the clamour of the idols in your heart. Don't be led by your desires. Be led by God at all times.

Chapter 7

DILIGENCE

And Ruth the Moabitess said unto Naomi, Let me now go to the field, and glean ears of corn after him in whose sight I shall find grace. And she said unto her, Go, my daughter.
Ruth 2:2

When Ruth and Naomi arrived in Israel, they settled down and prepared to adjust to living in their new home. It had been a while since Naomi and her family had left Israel and, as was expected, nothing was the same anymore. Sadly, while there was no husband or male relation to help assist, Naomi had chosen not to be a burden to her relatives. She knew about Boaz, a relative to her husband, but chose not to go to him begging.

After they had settled down, Ruth decided she needed to do something. She had no one. No one would do it for her. Naomi couldn't be expected to care for them both. She had to take personal responsibility for how her life turned out. An outcast in a foreign land, having learned about gleaning, she chose to find a place to stake a claim on what she believed she could possess. Choosing not to sit still and be idle, she got up, said her goodbyes to Naomi, searched out a field, and there worked very hard.

I have great respect for Ruth. She was extremely humble, sacrificial, loving, and caring, serving and not abandoning Naomi. She also proved to be a young lady of integrity, great intelligence and diligence, choosing to embrace the dignity of labour. Gleaning was belittling and demeaning, meant for the poor, involved living on what the rich left behind, and would be such hard labour beneath the sun for many hours (Was this what she left her family in Moab behind for?). Yet she chose it over begging.

Begging (sophisticated, overt, and covert) has become a lifestyle for so many. Let me be blunt. When you ask for something for which you have given no value in return or you cannot produce an invoice for, you are begging. You can call it 'asking', but chances are the person you are 'asking' from thinks you are begging. Ruth chose a different path.

Clearly, the role of diligence in the marketplace cannot be overemphasised.

I talked about diligence in the life of Rahab in the first book in this series and explored the important role it played in helping to move her from where she was to where she ought to be. Here again, we see it playing out in the life of Ruth.

Clearly, the role of diligence in the marketplace cannot be overemphasised.

Seest thou a man diligent in his business? he shall stand before kings; he shall not stand before mean men.
Prov. 22:29

Ruth worked so hard in the field, unashamed and uncaring of the opinions of others, and unaware the servants present were watching her.

And, behold, Boaz came from Bethlehem, and said unto the reapers, The LORD be with you. And they answered him, The LORD bless thee. Then said Boaz unto his servant that was set over the reapers, Whose damsel is this?

And the servant that was set over the reapers answered and said, It is the Moabitish damsel that came back with Naomi out of the country of Moab: And she said, I pray you, let me glean and gather after the reapers among the sheaves: so she came, and hath continued even from the morning until now, that she tarried a little in the house.
Ruth 2:4-7

When Boaz arrived and asked who she was, the servants didn't talk about how she was a beautiful woman or how great her personality was. They talked about what they had heard about her, now what they had seen, and how she worked all day only taking a little break. Not many might have known her personally. But that day, they left knowing she was a very hard worker, and this they told Boaz.

People are watching you. Beauty can get you noticed, but the value you bring to the table, diligence, and skill will bring you into a place of promotion. Almost no skill was required for gleaning, yet Ruth engaged it faithfully, working hard and diligently. God honoured the work of her hands and brought her before her king. When Jesus wanted to provide money for the taxes to be paid, he sent Peter to go do what he was already skilled at doing, fishing. The money was found in the mouth of the fish caught.

One of the ways provision comes from God is through the value you deliver. God will bless you through your skills as He did Peter and Ruth. You may need to acquire new skills or upskill. But start with what you have where you are today. There is something you can do.

Beauty can get you noticed, but the value you bring to the table, diligence, and skill will bring you into a place of promotion.

Those in full-time ministry deliver intangible spiritual value, and they are blessed with tangible gifts from those who can discern the intangible value which they deliver.

Let the elders that rule well be
counted worthy of double honour,

especially they who labour in the word and doctrine. For the scripture saith, Thou shalt not muzzle the ox that treadeth out the corn. And, The labourer is worthy of his reward.
1 Timothy 5:17

If we have sown unto you spiritual things, is it a great thing if we shall reap your carnal things?
1 Corinthians 9:11

This is legitimate and God-ordained. But the average working Christian does not fund his life this way, and it is to these I speak.

As you stay faithful and consistent in your marketplace delivering value, God Himself will orchestrate your meeting with your helper of destiny. Don't compare yourself with others. Don't be in a hurry. God has His eyes on you.

Chapter 8

THE POWER OF VISION

And he said, Blessed be thou of the LORD, my daughter: for thou hast shewed more kindness in the latter end than at the beginning, inasmuch as thou followedst not young men, whether poor or rich. And now, my daughter, fear not; I will do to thee all that thou requirest: for all the city of my people doth know that thou art a virtuous woman.
Ruth 3:10-11

Favour caused Ruth to select the right location. She didn't spend years gleaning and slaving away before stumbling on the right field. The field she chose was the exact field God wanted her assigned to. It would lead her to the promise.

Upon her arrival, however, her actions would determine if she would receive the promise or not. This is where vision is important. It is possible to be in the right location and miss God's blessings for you. A lack of vision has caused men to derail, to leave their place, to wander, to dwell where they shouldn't, and to think God is present when He has departed.

> And the water was *spent in the bottle, and she cast the child under one of the shrubs. And she went, and sat her down over against him a good way off, as it were a bowshot: for she said, Let me not see the death of the child. And she sat over against him, and lift up her voice, and wept.*
>
> *And God heard the voice of the lad; and the angel of God called to Hagar out of heaven, and said unto her, What aileth thee, Hagar? fear not; for God hath heard the voice of the lad where he is. Arise, lift up the lad, and hold him in thine hand; for I will make him a great nation.*
>
> *And God opened her eyes, and she saw a well of water; and she went, and filled the bottle with water, and gave the lad drink.*
> **Gen. 21:15-19**

A lack of vision has caused men to derail, to leave their place, to wander, to dwell where they shouldn't, and to think God is present when He has departed.

A lack of vision caused Hagar to place her son under a shrub to die when there was a well of water close by. A lack of vision caused Naomi to leave the house of bread along with her family and move to the land of Moab where all she experienced was loss. She came home empty.

A lack of vision caused Lot to leave the man he came out with, Abraham, in hopes of something better. He didn't recognise he was connected to a man who held the promise. He couldn't see who Abraham really was beyond a relative. As a result, he left him to seek his own way. He lost all he had in the destruction of Sodom and Gomorrah and had children born who were accursed by God – Ammon and Moab.

Ruth was in a foreign land where everything was new and different to her. She could have tried to learn the ways of the people, integrated herself into her new world the wrong way, and thought of ways to build her life by being 'smart'. But she stayed focused on the field, busy with her gleaning.

And she said, I pray you, let me glean and gather after the reapers among the sheaves: so she came, and hath continued even from the morning until now, that she tarried a little in the house.
Ruth 2:7

The Bible records that except for a short while where she rested, she worked tirelessly all day in the fields. The servants observed, noted her actions, and reported her to their leader, Boaz.

Many times, the first interface we will have with a king or with destiny will be through a servant. Naaman received his healing and became a new man from Elijah. This was possible through the slave girl in his household. Rebekah first met Eliezer at the well. He was representing Abraham, the father of the promise, and ultimately led her to become his son, Isaac's wife. Joseph met the chief butler in prison. Two years after his release, he remembered Joseph and brought him into his destiny through a meeting with Pharaoh.

Many times, the first interface we will have with a king or with destiny will be through a servant.

The servants Ruth met were young like she was and seemingly warm towards her. She could have given in to their advances if they made any, after all, they were more vibrant, approachable, and accessible than Boaz was. Besides, it would be a way for her to quickly gain her freedom from Naomi and build a new life. Yet, she chose to do nothing outside the instructions of her mother-in-law, honouring her mentor and coach.

Follow the Lord. Don't be led by sight or led away by inordinate desires. Sometimes when God is leading you, what you see may not look like it. I counsel that in all decisions, pray from a neutral standpoint until you are sure you have heard from God.

Chapter 9

REMEMBER NAOMI

And she took it up, and went into the city: and her mother in law saw what she had gleaned: and she brought forth, and gave to her that she had reserved after she was sufficed.
Ruth 2:18

The day was taking an unusual turn. Ruth sat among the servants and felt like she was in a dream. When she left home that morning, she hoped to get a little grain which she could share with Naomi. She never knew, before the end of the day, she would be sitting at a table with Boaz, served gifts by him, and fed to her heart's content. It was more than she imagined.

As she sat quietly, she took her meal and did two things which were remarkable and should serve as important lessons for each one of us as we navigate the marketplace.

EAT TO YOUR FILL

And Boaz said unto her, At mealtime come thou hither, and eat of the bread, and dip thy morsel in the vinegar. And she sat beside the reapers: and he reached her parched corn, and she did eat, and was sufficed...
Ruth 2:14

I know there are people, mothers especially, who are loving, caring, and always accessible to others. They are nurturers, encouragers, builders, and helpers. Despite having a heart of gold, always being sympathetic to the cause of another, and always caring for others please take a cue from Ruth.

Her full-time job was caring for her mother-in-law, serving, and working hard. She did this diligently and with all her heart. Yet, when the time came for her to eat, she sat down and ate to her fill. She knew if she was not nourished, she wouldn't have the strength to continue to serve, and both she and Naomi would be in trouble again.

Many of us do not 'feed' enough before beginning to serve others.

Many of us do not 'feed' enough before beginning to serve others. You cannot give what you don't have. You cannot feed others when you are empty. Feed yourself wholly. Feed your spirit, soul, and care for your body. Take care of your health. Be strong. When you are being pushed beyond your limits, you have the right to call a halt. Even in air flights, we are usually told to first put on our oxygen masks before trying to help others. You need to be alive and whole to function in your purpose and be a blessing to others. This can't be possible when you are ailing or dead.

Are you tired, weary, 'hungry'? Do your best to find the time to rest awhile, like Ruth did, and 'eat to your fill.'

BLESS THOSE WHO PAVED THE WAY

And she took it up, and went into the city: and her mother in law saw what she had gleaned: and she brought forth, and gave to her that she had reserved after she was sufficed.
Ruth 2:18

When Ruth was satisfied and had eaten to her fill, she kept what was left to take home to Naomi. When you are invited to palaces and given gifts, do you remember your Naomis? Some forget those who opened doors, gave them access, or connected them to helpers of destiny. There are some who give testimonies and cut out parts where they were helped by anyone!

Sadly, some of these recipients, when in need of another favour, return to the helpers again with no sense of shame. After a while, they soon wonder why those people are not so predisposed to helping them anymore. No one wants to feel used. These relationships thrive on gratitude and not on your ability to broker favours. Don't treat people like ladders. It is so wrong.

David, grandson to Ruth, was such a special individual. As we read his story, we see why he had such favour before God and men. When he needed to fight in the battle of Ziglag along with some of his men, he left some behind, those who were too tired and weary to continue, to stay back and protect what was left. Naturally, those who fought were disgruntled about sharing the spoils of war with those who stayed behind. David taught the men that both positions were important and one was not greater than the other. He also instituted a law to implement this decision:

Some forget those who opened doors, gave them access, or connected them to helpers of destiny.

> *For who will hearken unto you in this matter? but as his part is that goeth down to the battle, so shall his part be that tarrieth by the stuff: they shall part alike. And it was so from that day forward, that he made it a statute and an ordinance for Israel unto this day.*
> **1 Sam. 30:24–25**

When he was done with that, he didn't stop there. In the presence of his men who were still astounded by the new decree he had just passed and wondering at his rationale, he began to send out portions of the spoils to friends, families, elders, different cities, those who had cared for him in the years he spent wandering.

And when David came to Ziklag, he sent of the spoil unto the elders of Judah, even to his friends, saying, Behold a present for you of the spoil of the enemies of the LORD; To them which were in Bethel, and to them which were in south Ramoth, and to them which were in Jattir, And to them which were in Aroer, and to them which were in Siphmoth, and to them which were in Eshtemoa, And to them which were in Rachal, and to them which were in the cities of the Jerahmeelites, and to them which were in the cities of the Kenites, And to them which were in Hormah, and to them which were in Chorashan, and to them which were in Athach, And to them which were in Hebron, and to all the places where David himself and his men were wont to haunt.

1 Samuel 30:26-31

Do you remember those who gave you a helping hand when things weren't so rosy? Who prayed and interceded with you when things were rough? You are where you are because someone chose to help you. There is no one who is self-made on the face of the earth. It's a myth. Someone had to have helped you, given you a break, an introduction, or an opportunity. And you need to continue to acknowledge them.

Is it possible that Naomi was so stirred by the gifts she constantly received from Ruth that it unlocked a desire in her to bless Ruth?

Then Naomi her mother in law said unto her, My daughter, shall I not seek rest for thee, that it may be well with thee? And now is not Boaz of our kindred, with whose maidens thou wast? Behold, he winnoweth barley to night in the threshingfloor. Wash thyself therefore, and anoint thee, and put thy raiment upon thee, and get thee down to the floor: but make not thyself known unto the man, until he shall have done eating and drinking.

And it shall be, when he lieth down, that thou shalt mark the place where he shall lie, and thou shalt go in, and uncover his feet, and lay thee down; and he will tell thee what thou shalt do. And she said unto her, All that thou sayest unto me I will do.

Ruth 3:1-5

There is no one who is self-made on the face of the earth. It's a myth. Someone had to have helped you, given you a break, an introduction, or an opportunity. And you need to continue to acknowledge them.

Something stirred within Naomi, and suddenly a divine thought dropped in her head. I imagine she realised that Ruth could become Boaz's wife, a thought which may not even have crossed Ruth's mind. Naomi told Ruth, "Perfume yourself, put on new clothes. Don't tell anybody. Go to the threshing floor."

This was no coincidence. Naomi could only have been receptive to this thought because of the honour she had consistently received from Ruth. *Good understanding giveth favour... But the way of transgressors is hard. (Prov. 13:15)* If Ruth had not shown Naomi care when she had just received that sliver of opportunity, she may have preferred to keep Ruth by her side than let her be joined to Boaz. She knew from Ruth's precedence that if Ruth prospered, she also would prosper.

A river that forgets it source eventually dries up. It may not be immediate, but it invariably happens.

Note her language, "Shall I not seek rest for you?" It was a rhetorical question. *Is it not in my enlightened self-interest to help you, Ruth?* She gave instructions telling her what to do. When Ruth trusted Naomi and obeyed, in that instant access was given her to Boaz's heart and her place secured in his life.

Do not forget or despise those who paved the way for you. Do not be so focused on your journey and successes that you forget that faithful people held up your hands. A river that forgets its source eventually dries up. This may not be immediate, but it invariably happens.

SOW IN FAMINE

There are many who make the mistake of hoarding the little they have received in times of famine. However, the secret to getting out of famine is actually counterintuitive.

They that sow in tears shall reap in joy. He that goeth forth and weepeth, bearing precious seed, shall doubtless come again with rejoicing, bringing his sheaves with him.
Psalms 126:5-6

There is a mystery to sowing in tears that guarantees a harvest. When there is not enough, it is a sign that it is time to sow, irrespective of how much lack there is. This also guarantees there will be a harvest in the near future. If you don't, there would be even less or nothing to reap.

God promises that those who go forth weeping, bearing precious seed, will doubtless (undoubtedly, without a shadow of doubt) return rejoicing and bringing in sheaves with him. It is guaranteed.

Sow in famine. Get your clouds so heavy with rain that they have no choice than to pour out.

Chapter 10

IMPORTANT PROTOCOLS

And she lay at his feet until the morning: and she rose up before one could know another. And he said, Let it not be known that a woman came into the floor.
Ruth 3:14

We reach the final step in Ruth's story which she had to overcome to attain the promise. Every other principle I have shared some of us may be able to handle and consider easy. The only one which may seem tough is this final principle: keeping your mouth shut.

We see Ruth functioning discreetly as she went to where Boaz threshed grain in obedience to Naomi's instruction. But first, she would need to change her raiment.

OBSERVE THE PROTOCOL OF APPROACH

Wash thyself therefore, and anoint thee, and put thy raiment upon thee, and get thee down to the floor: but make not thyself known unto the man, until he shall have done eating and drinking.
Ruth 3:3

When Ruth was to go meet Boaz, the first instruction she received from Naomi was to wash, anoint herself and *change her raiment*. This was to be observed before the 'very important' assignment of meeting Boaz. Obedience to this instruction, irrespective of how fickle it was, would determine how receptive the one she was sent to would be.

We see this observed in scriptures by Joseph. Though he was an Israelite by birth, he had been sold as a slave by his brothers and brought to Egypt. The Israelites naturally had their hair and beards longer than usual, while the Egyptians, on the other hand, preferred to be clean-shaven and bald. When Joseph was invited to meet Pharaoh and help interpret his dream, his first choice wasn't to rush to the palace to carry out the 'important mission.' First, he took a detour.

Then Pharaoh sent and called Joseph, and they brought him hastily out of the dungeon: and he shaved himself, and changed his raiment, and came in unto Pharaoh.
Gen 41:14

The ability to 'change your raiment', putting off personal preconceived beliefs, traditions, personas to enter into or access what God has prepared for you cannot be emphasized. To derive value from anyone or any environment, there are protocols of approach you must understand and follow. Deriving value has to be on the terms of the helper, not the recipient.

Your ignorance or need would not give you access to the helpers you desire. Learn the protocol which those you seek to meet observe, and honour it.

The ability to 'change your raiment', putting off personal preconceived beliefs, traditions, personas to enter into or access what God has prepared for you cannot be emphasized.

LEARN TO BE SILENT

After Ruth had done all she could to look and smell good, she was to go to where Boaz was, making sure he didn't see her. She was not to disclose what she intended to him (or anyone else), but was to wait until he was done eating and drinking. It was only then she could tell him what she desired. When she obeyed, Boaz spoke with Ruth on the threshing-floor and entered into an agreement with her. But he told her one more thing: Tell no one.

In studying the life of Rahab in the first book in this series, we see her entering into an agreement with the spies, and just before they leave they tell her the same thing said to Ruth above: Tell no one.

Is this a coincidence? Is it not possible that despite the grandeur and confirmed assurances of promises made and agreements entered into in our lives today, many have not come to fruition because either of the parties concerned could not uphold this principle of silence? You shared it before it birthed and now there is nothing to show for it.

You shared it before it birthed and now there is nothing to show for it.

Learn silence. Learn when to speak. This is such an important key in the marketplace. Some have destroyed their deals by talking about transactions prematurely. Can a pregnancy be hidden? Why not let God complete what He has started?

Watch who you speak to. Your best friend may have a best friend who is not your friend. The friend you confide in might confide in a friend who is your enemy. It was Joseph's audience who put him in trouble. Like Ruth, wisely navigate each new terrain, eyes wide open, mouth shut, and learn to be discreet in all you do.

Chapter 11

THE PLACE OF FAVOUR

And Ruth the Moabitess said unto Naomi, Let me now go to the field, and glean ears of corn after him in whose sight I shall find grace. And she said unto her, Go, my daughter.
Ruth 2:2

As with many stories in the Bible and in the first book written in this series, *Rahab: Wisdom for Quantum Change,* we would discover a variety of values which might have endeared various individuals to God and made them candidates for His blessing. However, despite these traits which cannot be overlooked or underemphasised, we find one key attribute without which all striving would be vain. Without it, no one can fully become all God intends. Favour is this key attribute.

Many believe there is absolutely nothing you can do to find it. One just has it or it just happens. But entering into favour is actually based on certain principles. (You can learn more on this from my message on Esther on my YouTube channel).

Good understanding giveth favour: but the way of transgressors is hard.
Pro. 13:15

Favour shows up and answers to good understanding: a good understanding of how to relate to people with honour which is celebrating people for what they are and the attributes they possess while consciously overlooking what they are not. Knowing the difference in each is the precursor of honour. This is obviously what Ruth had to do or else she wouldn't have been able to last long with Naomi in the state she was in when our story opens. Favour and Wisdom are twin pillars needed to create quantum change.

Favour gives you access to privileges others struggle to receive. Favour singles you out from a crowd and causes you to be recognised while others go unseen. Favour was a huge factor in moving an undeserving slave from prison to becoming the prime minister of the head of an ancient civilisation, Egypt. Favour was what the Israelites had in the eyes of the Egyptians when they were to move out. Their efforts or struggles, talents and skills could not accomplish this. As a result,

Favour shows up and answers to good understanding.

the Egyptians gave them all they asked, even things that were not convenient.

Favour has nothing to do with looks and should not be mistaken for lust or attraction. Your beauty can also not bring you as far as favour can. There is a level of favour that makes struggles cease and this was a concept Ruth understood. Before leaving home, she talked about going to glean in a field where she would experience grace.

And Ruth the Moabitess said unto Naomi, Let me now go to the field, and glean ears of corn after him in whose sight I shall find grace. And she said unto her, Go, my daughter.
Ruth 2:2

Every step she turned, favour was activated to bring her into the place prepared by God for her. If I were to be asked what makes Ruth's story special I would say her understanding of the role of favour. In some of the verses where she spoke, the word favour or grace (a synonym) was a constant mention.

And Ruth the Moabitess said unto Naomi, Let me now go to the field, and glean ears of corn after him in whose sight I shall find **grace**. *And she said unto her, Go, my daughter.*
Ruth 2:2

Then she fell on her face, and bowed herself to the ground, and said unto him, Why have I found **grace**

in thine eyes, that thou shouldest take knowledge of me, seeing I am a stranger?
Ruth 2:10

Then she said, Let me find **favour** *in thy sight, my lord; for that thou hast comforted me, and for that thou hast spoken friendly unto thine handmaid, though I be not like unto one of thine handmaidens.*
Ruth 2:13

As a result of constantly expressing her desire for favour, things began to happen in line with all her words.

First, favour caused her not to wander aimlessly. Favour cut short her search. That same day, she suddenly found herself in a field that belonged to Boaz, a relation of Naomi her mother-in-law. This couldn't be a coincidence.

Favour and Wisdom are the twin pillars to create quantum change.

And she went, and came, and gleaned in the field after the reapers: and her hap was to light on a part of the field belonging unto Boaz, who was of the kindred of Elimelech.
Ruth 2:3

Secondly, of all the people in the field on that day, favour caused her to be noticed by Boaz himself. Was she the only woman on that field? She certainly wasn't. Yet on that day, he stopped long enough to notice and enquire about her.

And, behold, Boaz came from Bethlehem, and said unto the reapers, The LORD be with you. And they answered him, The LORD bless thee. Then said Boaz unto his servant that was set over the reapers, Whose damsel is this?
Ruth 2:4-5

Third, favour caused her to be noticed by the servants and to have a good report. Before you can receive access to a person of influence, almost every time, there would be someone whose opinion of you would be sought. When Boaz needed to know who she was, he didn't come to her directly. He spoke with the servants who had watched and interacted with her. That information was all he needed.

And the servant that was set over the reapers answered and said, It is the Moabitish damsel that came back with Naomi out of the country of Moab: And she said, I pray you, let me glean and gather after the reapers among the sheaves: so she came, and hath continued even from the morning until now, that she tarried a little in the house.
Ruth 2:6-7

Fourth, favour caused her to receive an introduction to Boaz, the man who was pivotal in God's plan for her life. He could have gone away after discovering who she was. But he, *immediately,* sent for her *and* showed her kindness.

Before you can receive access to a person of influence, almost every time, there would be someone whose opinion of you would be sought.

As a result of this introduction, she was no more to wander around gleaning in other fields but was to join his maidens on his field. Also, the harvesters were to intentionally leave shocks of grain for her to glean so she didn't have to work as hard. May favour cause your success not to come through difficult and endless labour!

Then said Boaz unto Ruth, Hearest thou not, my daughter? Go not to glean in another field, neither go from hence, but abide here fast by my maidens: Let thine eyes be on the field that they do reap, and go thou after them: have I not charged the young men that they shall not touch thee? and when thou art athirst, go unto the vessels, and drink of that which the young men have drawn. Then she fell on her face, and bowed herself to the ground, and said unto him, Why have I found grace in thine eyes, that thou shouldest take knowledge of me, seeing I am a stranger?
Ruth 2:8-10

Fifth, as she fell to her face thanking him and talking with him, he invited her to the meal table where she dined with him and his servants, and gave her enough to eat and take home.

And Boaz said unto her, At mealtime come thou hither, and eat of the bread, and dip thy morsel in the vinegar. And she sat beside the reapers: and he reached her parched corn, and she did eat, and was sufficed, and left.
Ruth 2:14

Sixth, favour caused Naomi to desire a better life for Ruth beyond serving and caring for her. There are many cases of people who serve for years in hopes that a reward would come from their employers or benefactors, and it never happens.

Then Naomi her mother in law said unto her, My daughter, shall I not seek rest for thee, that it may be well with thee? And now is not Boaz of our kindred, with whose maidens thou wast? Behold, he winnoweth barley to night in the threshingfloor. Wash thyself therefore, and anoint thee, and put thy raiment upon thee, and get thee down to the floor: but make not thyself known unto the man, until he shall have done eating and drinking.
Ruth 3:1-3

Favour caused Ruth to be remembered by Naomi after a while of living with her, who suddenly awoke to the fact that she might have a bigger role to play in Ruth's life than as her co-living mother-in-law. As a result, she gave divine instructions that changed Ruth's life.

Seventh, favour caused Ruth's request to be redeemed by Boaz to be granted by him immediately she obeyed Naomi. She could have despised Naomi's instructions, afterall, she was the one working on the fields with Boaz and knew to an extent what was or wasn't acceptable. Yet, she honoured and trusted Naomi enough to obey her. Within 24 hours she was betrothed to Boaz.

Tarry this night, and it shall be in the morning, that if he will perform unto thee the part of a kinsman, well; let him do the kinsman's part: but if he will not do the part of a kinsman to thee, then will I do the part of a kinsman to thee, as the LORD liveth: lie down until the morning.
Ruth 3:13

Honour brings favour.

May favour cause your success not to come through difficult and endless labour!

Eighth, favour caused her to receive conception from the Lord and to become a mother.

So Boaz took Ruth, and she was his wife: and when he went in unto her,

the LORD gave her conception, and she bare a son. And the women said unto Naomi, Blessed be the LORD, which hath not left thee this day without a kinsman, that his name may be famous in Israel.
Ruth 4:13-14

And the women her neighbours gave it a name, saying, There is a son born to Naomi; and they called his name Obed: he is the father of Jesse, the father of David.
Ruth 4:17

Ruth wasn't just a mother to a random child but to Obed who would be the grandfather to David. What a God!

Finally, favour caused her to be grafted into the lineage of Jesus.

The book of the generation of Jesus Christ, the son of David, the son of Abraham. … And Salmon begat Booz of Rachab; and Booz begat Obed of Ruth; and Obed begat Jesse…
Matthew 1:1, 5

A stranger from Moab, a widow in a strange land, would be written into the genealogy of The Christ! What a story. That's the God we serve.

Everything we read above about Ruth's life was enveloped by favour. By wisdom and her exemplary traits, genuine love, honour, sacrifice, the fact that she also honoured the unfavourable Naomi, she activated favour and we see God lavishing her over and over with His goodness.

Is this possible for us too? Thankfully, yes! Thanks to God for the new covenant which gives us access to God's blessings and the fullness of His grace through His son Jesus.

For thou, LORD, wilt bless the righteous; with favour wilt thou compass him as with a shield.
Psalms 5:12

As children of the new birth, we are the righteousness of God in Christ Jesus. Acknowledge, appropriate, and walk in it.

Chapter 12

REJECTION

And Ruth said, Intreat me not to leave thee, or to return from following after thee: for whither thou goest, I will go; and where thou lodgest, I will lodge: thy people shall be my people, and thy God my God.
Ruth 1:16

Isn't it amazing that Naomi thought the story of her life was over? She didn't know that in returning to Israel, she was entering into a second season of her life. She would become surrogate mother to Ruth whose life would play out God's script.

Isn't it interesting that Naomi, who was of the chosen people of God and had an existing covenant with the One who was sure to stand by His children, felt like a reject? On the other hand Ruth, who had no earthly hope of ever deriving any benefit from Jehovah, knowing she was a complete stranger in a strange city, an outcast from the covenant and cursed, was positive about starting over and stepping into the future.

Rejection is a word which plagues many in our world today. It is the tool used by the enemy to cause many to give up on going on, doing more, becoming all God has designed they should be. There are too many disheartened believers like Naomi. She said "God has rejected me", "God has testified against me." What she really meant was "God has despised me. God has made me small. I went away full. God was the one who brought me back empty." Was it God who brought her back empty? Her pain caused her, along with many children of God, to be disillusioned and distorted her view of who God really is. Like many, she had adjusted her theology to fit her experiences and crafted a God in the image of her sufferings and experiences.

Like many, she had adjusted her theology to fit her experiences and crafted a God in the image of her sufferings and experiences.

This is what many do when they are tired of failing over and over, and when their experiences of God do not seem to line up with what they see in the Word. It is difficult to keep being held liable for failing, so after a while, they need to redefine God as the culprit. I say this to those who have not had things go the way you expected, are in pain, have lost something or someone. Those who are angry with God. I have news for you. Make up with Him. Go to Him and tell Him how angry and hurt you are. That's the best way.

The time has come to call yourself to a conference, and to say "I have failed. I have been defeated. It hasn't gone the way I planned. But will I leave it this way?" At the end of the day, we must say to Jesus the same words Peter did,

Then Simon Peter answered him, Lord, to whom shall we go? thou hast the words of eternal life.
John 6:68

When you pour out your heart to God and you quieten down before Him, He begins to communicate His word and heart to you through various ways.

There are also those who, though children of the covenant under Jesus, may feel their natural heritage has caused them to be rejected like Ruth had been. She also had to bear the curse and rejection placed on Moab by God, not for something she had done, but for things that occurred years before she existed. I don't know what your family has done which you carry around and causes you to feel rejected. Jesus Christ has given you the way out. You bear only His liberty. Nothing else. The key to living free is ultimately in your hands.

When you pour out your heart to God and you quieten down before Him, He begins to communicate His word and heart to you through various ways.

Ruth said with her actions, *God, you might decide to have rejected me, but I am not rejecting you. It might look like you have dealt with me. I have lost a husband. I have suffered loss. But I have nowhere else to go but to you again.* Once you take this posture and do not reject yourself, God has a plan waiting for you. Like her, your story is not over until you decide it is over. I move further to say it is not over until you have victory.

Here's my prayer for you as spoken by God to David:

> *Pursue: for thou shalt surely overtake them, and without fail recover all.*
> **1 Sam 30:8**

About the Author

Olajumoke Adenowo (Arc) is a multiple award-winning architect with over three decades of industry experience. Described as Africa's 'Starchitect' and trailblazer when profiled by CNN and BBC, she is one of Africa's outstanding architects and the only female in this elite category. Christened the **Face of Architecture in Nigeria** by the Guardian, she has been featured in the world's foremost architectural journal Architectural Record and in Forbes Women and Fortune magazine.

In 2013, she was instituted into the Hall of Fame of **Personalities of Black Ancestry** by the University of West England, Bristol, among other global personalities of black heritage.

Olajumoke gained admission into Obafemi Awolowo University, Ile-Ife, at the age of fourteen, and she acquired the first distinction in Masters of Science in Architecture in the University's history. She is also an alumnus of a number of prestigious institutions including the Harvard Kennedy School of Government, the Yale School of Management, the IESE Business School amongst others. She is a member of the Institute of Chartered Arbitrators (UK) and a Fellow of the Nigerian Institute of Architects.

Olajumoke started her career at Femi Majekodunmi Associates, where she had the privilege of designing the Federal Ministry of Finance Headquarters in Abuja. In 1994, she founded her own multi-award-winning architecture firm, AD Consulting, which specialises also in the master planning of eco-sensitive developments. AD Consulting is Nigeria's most internationally awarded firm. She has been the principal partner from inception till date.

In 1999, Olajumoke's passion for raising transformational leaders led her to establish the faith-based philanthropy, Awesome Treasures Foundation. It is recognized by the United Nations and affiliated to the Edmond De Rothschild Foundation Family Philanthropy Platform. Awesome Treasures Foundation is established on three continents with initiatives impacting millions.

She is the pioneer recipient of the **New African Women in Business Award**, has been recognised as one of Africa's '**Top Ten Most Powerful Women in Business**', one of **Nigeria's Most Inspiring Women**, one of Nigeria's **100 most Influential Nigerians**, the International Alliance for Women **World of Difference 100 Award**, as well as one of the **Most Inspiring Women in Nigeria** amongst other honours.

Olajumoke Adenowo was the recipient of the **2019 Leadership Award** by the Constituency For Africa (Washington, DC). In 2019 she was appointed a visiting professor at Germany's Leading Architecture program, Technische Universitat Munchen (TUM) in Germany. She was honoured as a Laureate and Guest Scientist at the Chair of Theory, History of Architecture and Art & Design.

Adenowo is a speaker of note at summits and conferences, and has spoken at several global platforms, including the Global Women's Forum, Harvard Business School's Africa Business Club, Cambridge University's African Society, and SOLVE MIT's flagship conference for global thought leaders and innovators. She is also a minister of the gospel, and member of The International Coalition of Apostolic Leaders. She ministers to all genders and also young adults, raising transformational leaders, and has held over 120 Awesome Treasures Summits internationally, with attendees of up to 5000 at the youth summits.

Olajumoke has served on juries and panels of global initiatives such as The Cartier Initiative for Women Awards. She has authored several books, including *Life Spring, Mysterious Seed*, *Appointment With Destiny*, and *Beyond My Dreams*, and hosts her own syndicated radio program, Voice of Change on Leadership.

She is married to Olukorede and they are blessed with two men.